The Official

m&m's® BRAND

History of the

Calendar

AD 3 - AD 4 - AD 5

• Larry Dane Brimner •
illustrated by Karen E. Pellaton

3002200069415W

Charlesbridge

To Sheila Cole, Jean Ferris, and Kathy Krull—writers for a new millennium
–L. D. B.

To my favorite filmmaker, Gretchen
–K. E. P.

Text © 2002 by Larry Dane Brimner
Illustrations © 2002 by Karen E. Pellaton
All rights reserved, including the right of
reproduction in whole or in part in any form.

Published by Charlesbridge Publishing
85 Main Street
Watertown, MA 02472
(617) 926-0329
www.charlesbridge.com

Printed in South Korea
(hc) 10 9 8 7 6 5 4 3 2 1
(sc) 10 9 8 7 6 5 4 3 2 1

™/® M&M'S, M and the M&M'S Characters are trademarks
of Mars, Incorporated or its affiliates.
© Mars, Inc. 2002.
Manufactured and distributed under
license by Charlesbridge Publishing.

Library of Congress Cataloging-in-Publication Data
Brimner, Larry Dane.
The official "M&M's"® brand history of the calendar /
Larry Dane Brimner; illustrated by Karen E. Pellaton.
p.   cm.
Summary: Traces the history and uses of various calendars,
from the Chinese calendar, introduced in 2637 B.C., to the
Gregorian calendar of today.
ISBN 1-57091-431-1 (reinforced for library use)
ISBN 1-57091-432-X (softcover)

1. Calendar —History—Juvenile literature. [1. calendar.] I.
Title: Official M&M's brand history of the calendar. II.
Title. Official M and M's brand history of the calendar. III.
Pellaton, Karen E., ill. IV. Title.
CE6 .B75 2002
529'.3—dc21   2001004826

The illustrations in this book were done in watercolor on
Arches watercolor paper "hot press."
The display type and text type were set in Futura, Publicity
Gothic, and Stone Informal.
Color separations were made by Sung In Printing, Inc.,
South Korea.
Printed and bound by Sung In Printing, Inc.,
South Korea
Production supervision by Brian G. Walker
Designed by Diane M. Earley

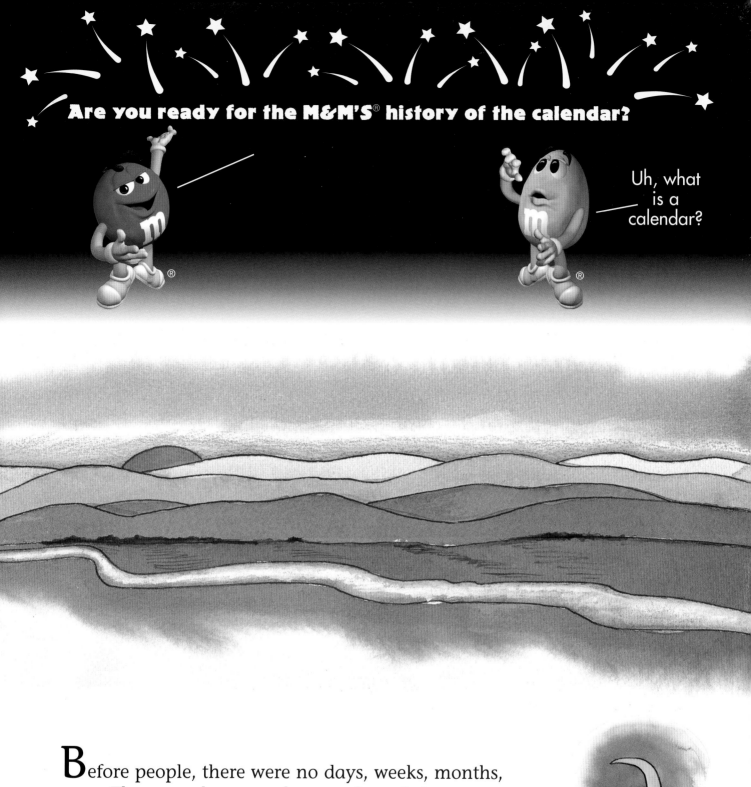

Are you ready for the M&M'S® history of the calendar?

Uh, what is a calendar?

Before people, there were no days, weeks, months, or years. Then people came along and needed to measure time. We've been doing it ever since.

Some small amounts of time were easy to decide on and understand. A day was the time from one sunrise or sunset to the next. The time between market days became what we now call a week. Months changed with the return of the new moon. A year? Usually this was the time from one spring to the next, from one fall to the next, or in Egypt, from one flood to the next.

But how do we know what year it is?

Can you remember everything you did yesterday or last week, or do you forget some things? Imagine trying to keep track of an event that happened 50, 100, or 1000 years ago. People need to remember the past and plan for the future, and so they count the years.

CHINESE CALENDAR FOR THE YEAR 4698

To keep track, people invented *calendars*. But calendars start at different times. The Chinese calendar is one of the longest-running calendars in history. Emperor Huangdi introduced it in 2637 B.C.

What's B.C.?

Before candy?

The Islamic calendar began in A.D. 622—a way of remembering Mohammed's journey from Mecca to Medina. As a result, in 2000, the year of the new millennium, the Muslim calendar reached the year 1420.

The Hebrew calendar counts from what the Jewish people historically believed to be the time of creation—a date even earlier than the beginning of the Chinese calendar. The result? The year 2010 will be the Hebrew year 5770.

B.C. and A.D.

Many years ago, a Catholic monk had been given the task of figuring out when Jesus was born. When he gave his report to the pope, he added the words *anno Domini* ("in the year of our Lord") to a date that he had counted from the birth of Jesus—which the monk figured to be some five hundred years before. Since then, that Latin phrase has been abbreviated by writing A.D. to symbolize any date after the birth of Jesus. The abbreviation B.C. stands for "before Christ."

Today there are about forty different calendars in use around the world, usually to mark religious holy days and traditional festivals. No single one is more correct than the others because each serves its own purpose, but so many calendars could be confusing. You wouldn't have wanted to get on a plane in New York in the year 2002 and arrive in China in the year 4700! That's why almost everyone uses the same calendar.

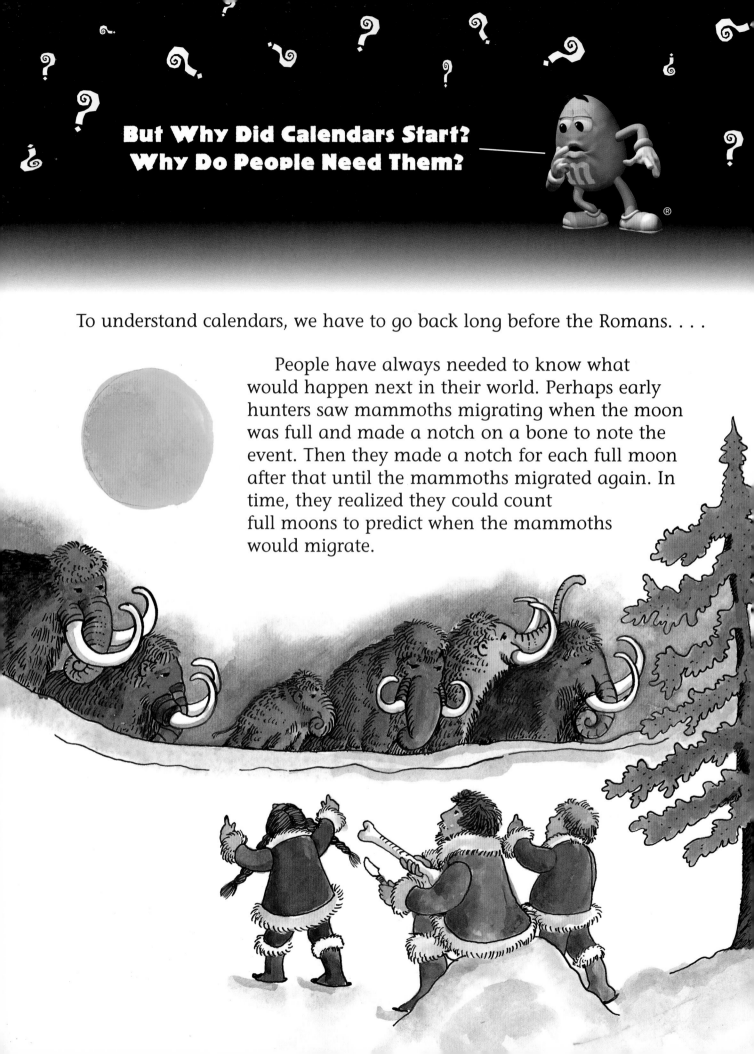

But Why Did Calendars Start? Why Do People Need Them?

To understand calendars, we have to go back long before the Romans. . . .

People have always needed to know what would happen next in their world. Perhaps early hunters saw mammoths migrating when the moon was full and made a notch on a bone to note the event. Then they made a notch for each full moon after that until the mammoths migrated again. In time, they realized they could count full moons to predict when the mammoths would migrate.

Other "calendars" might have counted the moons from one winter to the next. These simple calendars helped people plan their lives.

All that counting and they didn't even have "M&M'S"® to help them.

Later, when people started to farm, farmers and merchants carried their crops and goods to market. It did them no good if they arrived the day after market day. People needed to measure time with accurate calendars to track the days and months and years.

Let's Make a Calendar—It Sounds Easy!

Yeah, but there are a few problems.

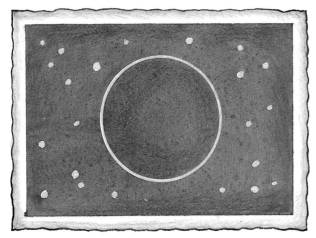

A new moon—a time when we cannot see sunlight on the moon.

The earliest calendars we know about followed the *lunar* cycle. Each new moon signaled the beginning of a new month.

The Babylonians (in what is now Iraq) soon discovered a small problem with a lunar calendar: It didn't stay lined up with the seasons. If it didn't, they might plant at the wrong time. So, by 432 B.C. they were using a new calendar that was sometimes twelve months long and sometimes thirteen months long. It was complicated, but it worked . . . until somebody couldn't remember if they should be using the twelve-month or thirteen-month calendar.

Accuracy wasn't the only problem with early calendars. Even then the calendars were different! Some places started each new year on the spring equinox—around March 21, when the number of hours of daylight equals the number of hours of darkness. But in Egypt the new year began in the middle of June. On top of that, some places began their day at sunset, while others began it at sunrise or midday. It must have been very confusing for travelers!

Sirius

Canis Major

At least they didn't have jet lag back in those days!

The Egyptians were the first to make a lunar calendar work better. Around 4000 B.C., they began to use a notched reed to measure the high-water mark of the Nile River—and discovered that the floods happened almost exactly one year apart. Then Egyptian priest-astronomers noticed that Sirius, the dog star, appeared in the predawn sky at the same time as the flood.

At the first sight of these two yearly events, priest-astronomers would declare a new year of three seasons: flooding, seed time, and harvest. And the count of months would begin again.

Most lunar calendars didn't follow the seasons at all. They alternated 6 months of 29 days each with 6 months of 30 days each. This added up to a year of 354 days.

One orbit of the earth around the sun = one solar year

But the earth's tilt and its orbit around the sun make the seasons. A complete orbit—one year by the *solar* calendar—takes a little longer than 365 days. So, a lunar year of 354 days is 11 days short of a solar year. This meant that when people used a lunar calendar, months slowly drifted away from their original seasons. Eventually, "planting time" according to the calendar would be in the winter.

To fix the lunar calendars, people added extra days or stuck an extra month into the calendar every few years.

They should have asked <u>me</u> for help.

The Chinese

Hey, this calendar works pretty well!

The Chinese found a way to combine the lunar calendar with the solar year. Their lunisolar calendar began months on the new moon but added extra months every two or three years to stay in agreement with the seasons. This calendar is still in use.

Like many people, the Chinese saw pictures among the stars. They named their constellations after animals: rat, ox, tiger, hare, dragon, snake, horse, sheep, monkey, rooster, dog, and pig. Each animal influences the year it rules over. The year 2000 (year 4698 on the Chinese calendar) was the year of the dragon, a time of excitement and complexity.

PRE-COLUMBIAN AMERICANS

Can you imagine what their watches looked like?

Read this sentence in twos, left to right, top to bottom.

Introduction glyph

9 bak'tuns

Zero k'atuns

19 tuns

2 winals

4 k'ins

260 day Venus calendar day: 2 k'an

A 9-day calendar day is here

The moon's calendar begins here with...

...the name of the god of the night and the age of the current moon.

It's the third lunar month

It's the 29th day of the third lunar month

The solar month is 2 Yax

The verb comes next: it's "burned incense."

This is the name of the king and this is the name of his new temple.

No one knows when Native Americans, who live in what is now Mexico and Central American, first started using calendars. But the ancient Maya perfected a complex calendar system that kept track of the cycles of the sun, the moon, Venus, as well as the number of days that had passed since the beginning of time. Each day had its own omens and fortunes, so birthdays were very important. The date shown here was carved onto a sculpture recording a day when a Maya king dedicated a new temple by burning incense.

The first part of this sentence begins with the number of days since the beginning of time. It starts with the longest time period first, a kind of mega-century called the *bak'tun*. A *k'in* is one day. There are twenty *k'ins* in a *winal*, 19 *winals* to a *tun*, 360 *k'ins* in a *tun*. *Tuns* are almost like our year. There are 20 *tuns* in each k'atun, 20 k'atuns to a *bak'tun* or 400 *tuns* make a *bak'tun*. After the date comes the verb, then the subject, then the object. The Maya still use these calendars today.

The Maya wrote the number one as a dot and five as a bar. Their zero looks like a half-flower with three petals. The number twenty is written as a rectangle with three circles and three dots.

THE ROMANS

What about the calendar used in most of the world today? That smooth-running calendar comes from the Roman calendar, which in its early days did not run smoothly at all. Long ago, the Romans had an awkward ten-month year, less than three hundred days long. Around 700 B.C., they tried to make it work better by adding two months—Januarius and Februarius—and an extra day.

Wow, they just made it up as they went along!

Did this work? A twelve-month year was better than a ten-month year, but its 355 days still fell short of the solar year. What we call September didn't stay in the fall. So the Romans tried to fix that problem by adding an extra month to the end of February.

This could have worked, except it wasn't carefully managed. Rulers and priests added the extra month for their own gain—usually to stay in office longer.

NOTICE
COMING SOON!
ONE EXTRA MONTH

COMING ONE EXTRA MONTH

COMING ONE EXTRA MONTH

Red-Letter Days
Special days in the eight-day Roman week were shown in red letters on the calendar. Some people think this is where we get our own term "Red-Letter Days." What do you think?

I think they named them after me!

After these "fixes," the Roman calendar soon got out of step again with the seasons. It took Julius Caesar to really fix it. War took him to Egypt, where he fell in love with the Egyptian queen, Cleopatra—and helped her take the Egyptian throne away from her brother.

Finally, some interesting trivia!

In Egypt, Caesar learned about the solar calendar the Egyptians used. Right away, he decided that the Roman Empire should use one, too.

People resist change, but Caesar was a powerful man. It's a good thing, too, because to make the new calendar work he had to do some bold things. First, he established 12 alternating months of 30 and 31 days. February had 29 days, but got an extra day every fourth year—a "leap year."

Once in a Blue Moon
Ever hear the expression "once in a blue moon"? Originally, it meant something that was very rare. That's because the moon only looks blue if there's a lot of dust or smoke in the air . . . say when a large volcano erupts. Recently, people started to use it to mean another rarity—the second full moon when a month has two.

Looks like rush hour!

Next, Caesar made the year 46 B.C. longer by more than two months. He had to, to bring the calendar back in step with the seasons. This turned the Roman world topsy-turvy: Shipping schedules were interrupted, contracts were disputed, and taxes were protested. Caesar's 445-day year, the longest in history, became "the Year of Confusion."

In the end, it worked. Rome finally had a calendar that kept pace with the seasons and was easy to manage. It was solar, almost identical to the Egyptian calendar. Later, the Roman Senate decided to honor Caesar by changing Quinctilis (the seventh month) to Julius. Imagine—if it weren't for Caesar, we wouldn't have July!

After Caesar's death his great-nephew Augustus came to power and wanted a month named after himself, too. He chose one that had been lucky for him. But it was only a 30-day month, and Caesar's month had 31 days. So Augustus took a day from February. That gave us August, but now poor February was left with only 28 days.

So they called this the Julian calendar—not bad, to get a calendar named after you!

QUINCTILIS
JULIUS

SEXTILIS
AUGUSTUS

The Julian calendar came close to working, but it was eleven minutes off the solar year. By 1582—long after the Roman Empire had ended—eleven minutes each year had added up to about ten days. Easter, a spring festival, might be celebrated in the wrong season!

To fix things, Pope Gregory XIII declared that October 5 would become October 15. Ten days were gone forever.

The pope also changed Caesar's leap-year rule. Every fourth year would still be a leap year, and years ending in 00 that could be evenly divided by 400 would be leap years, too. But if they could not be evenly divided by 400, they would have the usual 365 days. As a result, the year 2000 was a leap year, but 1900 was not.

The *Gregorian calendar* was adopted gradually all over the rest of the world. As time goes by, it will have to be corrected again; by 4909, it will be one whole day off.

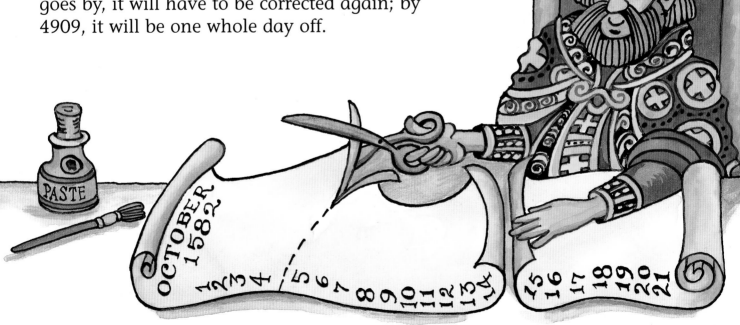

"Give Us Back Our Eleven Days"

The Pope's influence extended far and wide, but not into countries like Germany and England. These continued to use the Julian calendar. But 170 years later, England and its colonies finally started to use the Gregorian calendar—and they were among the last to do it.

By then, the date according to the English calendar was eleven days different from the rest of Europe. So, the English dropped them out of the calendar—Wednesday, September 2, 1752, was followed by Thursday, September 14. Some people thought the eleven days had been stolen from their lives! Employers refused to pay a full month's wages, landlords wanted a full month's rent, and mobs rioted in the streets. "Give us back our eleven days!" they cried.

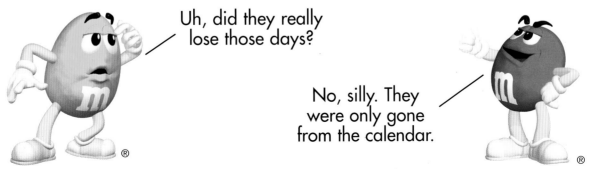

Uh, did they really lose those days?

No, silly. They were only gone from the calendar.

TIME, WORDS,

People have often needed to keep track of larger amounts of time, too, and invented words for them. Today, we call 10 years a decade. A person who is 10 years old is also 1 decade old. A century is 10 decades, or 100 years.

And we say 1,000 years is one millennium.

I'm all out of fingers.

These words have roots in other languages. Decade came from the Greek deka, meaning "ten." Century and millennium came from the Romans, who spoke Latin: centuria, meaning "a group of one hundred," and mill, meaning "one thousand."

We also borrowed something else from the Romans: Roman numerals. Sometimes they are still carved into cornerstones of public buildings to mark the year they were built.

What Roman numeral might you find in the cornerstone of a building built in the year 2000? MM—the mark of the new millennium, a move from the 1000s to the 2000s.

MM—Look, that's us!

ACME
BUILDING
MM

AND NUMBERS

MM is a tidy way to write the year 2000, but Roman numerals are not always tidy.

MM=2000

It's GREEK to me.

Actually it's ROMAN.

The longest year so far, in the number of Roman numerals, was 1888: MDCCCLXXXVIII. Thirteen numerals long!

ROMAN NUMERALS

Roman numerals are letters of the alphabet that stand for numbers:

I (1), V (5), X (10), L (50),
C (100), D (500), M (1000).

The letters are strung together to add up to a number. Like this:

II = 2 (1 + 1)   VII = 7 (5 + 1 + 1)
        XXX = 30 (10 + 10 + 10)
IX = 9 (10 - 1)   MM = 2000 (1000 + 1000)

Why isn't the number 9 written as VIIII (5 + 1 + 1 + 1 + 1)?

No one knows for sure, but there are rules that apply to all Roman numerals:

- Always start with the biggest numeral possible.
- Numerals to the right of a bigger one are added. So VIII (5 + 1 + 1 + 1) equals 8.
- The numeral on the left of a bigger one is subtracted. So IX (10 - 1) equals 9.
- A numeral may be repeated only three times in a row.

So That's How It All Happened!

We have the Gregorian calendar,
and we've reached a millennium!

But what's the big deal?

Why *were* people so excited about a new millennium?
It may have to do with our number system, which goes back
to India over one thousand years ago. People there were the
first to use a number system of nine digits plus zero.

Now, ten and its multiples seem important to us.
A tenth, twentieth, or thirtieth birthday is a milestone
event. So is watching your car's odometer roll over to
50,000 or 100,000 miles. These things happen only once.
So it is with a millennium—10 centuries,
100 decades, 10 times 10 times 10 years!

1-2-3-4-5-6-7-8-9

Indian numbers
became what we now
call "Arabic numerals."
We still use them today,
because they are easier to work
with than Roman numerals.

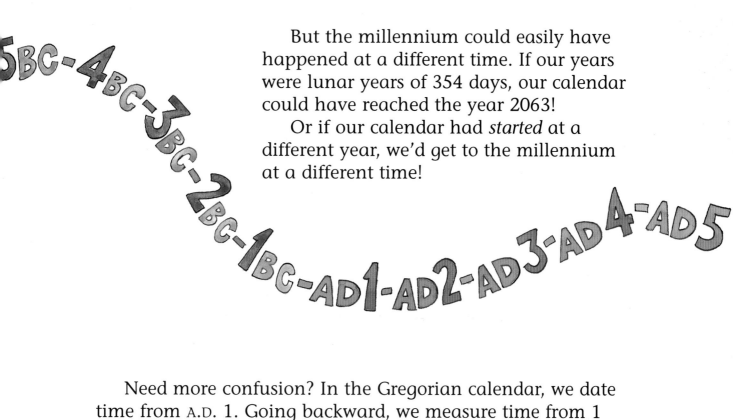

But the millennium could easily have happened at a different time. If our years were lunar years of 354 days, our calendar could have reached the year 2063!

Or if our calendar had *started* at a different year, we'd get to the millennium at a different time!

Need more confusion? In the Gregorian calendar, we date time from A.D. 1. Going backward, we measure time from 1 B.C. There was no "zero" year. So, A.D. 1 through A.D. 1000 was the first millennium. By this countdown, the third millennium began on January 1, 2001, and not the year 2000.

Does it matter? Well, most people decided that the millennium would start on the day when the nines turn into zeroes—when 1999 turned into 2000.

I get it! Calendars are inventions—and people keep changing them.

Right! And different places have different calendars.

And different celebrations.

When the Millennium Is Over, What Comes Next?

Look back at the second millennium. Were there any changes? You bet. The second millennium changed in ways that people in the first millennium never expected. The invention of movable type and, much later, the computer, influenced the spread of information. The combustion engine and air flight had a profound impact on the way people work and travel. Rockets have allowed us to explore other worlds.

Some Second Millennium Inventions:

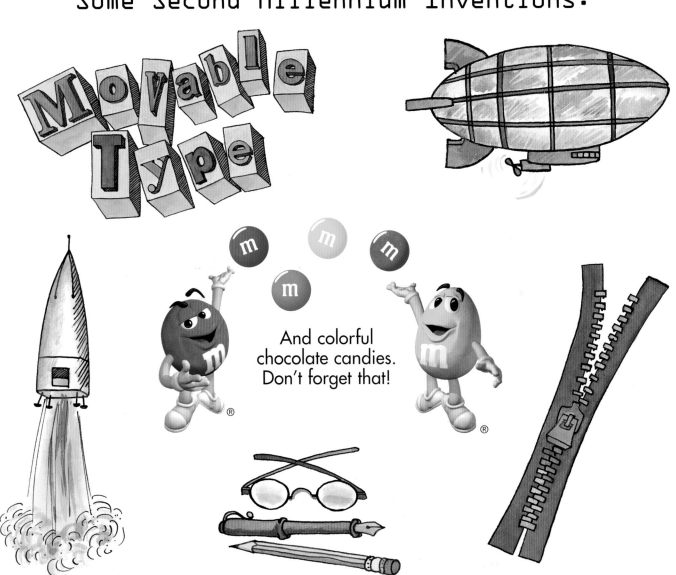

And colorful chocolate candies. Don't forget that!

What lies ahead? No one knows for sure. But there will be changes. Are you surprised?

By the year 3000, the world will have changed in ways that we cannot imagine today. But one thing is certain. People will continue to measure time—just as they always have.

The Millennium Clock

To encourage people to think about time beyond the millennium and about the long-term future of the Earth, some people are planning a millennium clock. It won't count seconds and minutes, like a regular clock. Instead, the millennium clock will tick off centuries. And rather than chiming on the hour, it will chime each millennium . . . for the next 10,000 years.

It will be a reminder that our Earth was here long before people walked its continents . . . long before people began inventing and using calendars . . . and will likely be here far into the future—if we plan for it.

A year can seem like a long time when you are waiting for your next birthday. But is it? What about a decade? A decade is longer. So is a century. And a millennium—a thousand years—is the longest time of all . . .

. . . unless you consider that the earth has been around a lot longer than that. The earth is about 4.5 billion years old—that's about 4.5 million millennia! So scientists measure the age of the earth in geologic time. They invented eons (the longest divisions of geologic time) and eras (at least two to an eon) and periods (shorter than an era) and epochs (shorter than a period, but still thousands and thousands of years long).

So, given the big picture, a millennium isn't such a long time after all. It's just a few candles on Earth's enormous cake.

Bibliography

Apfel, Necia H. *Calendars*. New York: Franklin Watts, 1985.

Dale, Rodney. *Timekeeping*. London: The British Library, 1992.

Evenson, A. E. *About the History of the Calendar*. Chicago: Children's Press, 1972.

Fakih, Kimberly Olson. *Off the Clock: A Lexicon of Time Words and Expressions*. Boston: Houghton Mifflin, 1995.

Mandell, Muriel. *Simple Experiments in Time with Everyday Materials*. New York: Sterling Publishing, 1997.

Older, Jules. *Telling Time: How to Tell Time on Digital and Analog Clocks!* Watertown: Charlesbridge, 2000.

WWW Resources

National Institute of Standards and Technology. "A Walk through Time." *Provides information and illustrations of ancient calendars from the Egyptians to the Babylonians to the Maya.*
http://physics.nist.gov/GenInt/Time/ancient.html

Institute of Dynamic Educational Advancement. "Calendars through the Ages." *Follows the development of the modern calendar and delves into other calendars still in use today. A section on ancient calendars provides useful information and is accompanied by photographs.*
http://webexhibits.org/calendars/calendar.html

World Book. "Calendars: Counting the Days." *The editors at World Book have compiled information on what defines a calendar, how to measure time, and modern and ancient calendars.*
http://www.worldbook.com/fun/calendars/html/calendars.htm.

It's been lovely learning with you!